THE ODYSSEY
HOMER

Abridged and adapted by Mark Falstein
Illustrated by Karen Locisano

A PACEMAKER CLASSIC

GLOBE FEARON
Pearson Learning Group

Project Editors: Ann Clarkson and Ayanna Taylor
Senior Editor: Lynn Kloss
Designer: Lisa Nuland
Production Editor: Travis Bailey
Composition: Phyllis Rosinsky
Illustrator: Karen Locisano

ISBN 0-835-93589-2
Printed in the United States of America

7 8 9 10 11   05

1-800-321-3106
www.pearsonlearning.com

Contents

Cast of Characters

People:

Odysseus	king of Ithaca, a Greek island
Penelope	Odysseus' wife
Telemachus	son of Odysseus and Penelope
Antinous	one of Penelope's suitors
Eurymachus	one of Penelope's suitors
Amphinomus	one of Penelope's suitors
Leodes	one of Penelope's suitors
Eurycleia	a servant in Odysseus' palace
Nausicaa	a Phaeacian princess
Alcinous	king of the Phaeacians; Nausicaa's father
Arete	wife of Alcinous; Nausicaa's mother
Eurylochus	a man in Odysseus' crew
Eumaeus	a swineherd (pig farmer) and loyal servant of Odysseus

Gods, Goddesses, Spirits, and Monsters:

Zeus	king of the gods on Mount Olympus
Athena	goddess of wisdom; Zeus' daughter
Poseidon	god of the sea and of earthquakes
Hermes	messenger of the gods; he also guides human souls to the land of the dead
Calypso	a nymph (half-goddess) who loves Odysseus
Polyphemus	a Cyclops (one-eyed giant)
Circe	another nymph
Ghost of Tiresias	a seer (person who tells the future)

The Story So Far

The Odyssey is a sequel. It is the second of Homer's two great epic poems. To understand the story better, it helps to know something about "part one," *The Iliad.*

The Iliad is the story of the Trojan War. This war might actually have taken place around 1250 B.C. *The Iliad,* however, is not a history. It is a tale of myth and magic. The gods and goddesses of ancient Greece are important characters. They take sides in the war and help the human characters.

According to myth, the war started this way: Paris was a prince of the city of Troy. Three goddesses asked him to judge who among them was the most beautiful. Aphrodite, the goddess of love, offered Paris a reward if he chose her. He could have Helen, the most beautiful woman in the world. However, Helen was married to Menelaus. He was the king of Sparta, a city in Greece. When Paris visited Sparta, Aphrodite made Helen fall in love with him. Helen ran away with Paris. Menelaus and his brother, Agamemnon, led a Greek army against Troy to bring her back. The war that followed is called the Trojan War after the name *Troy.*

The Iliad takes place during the last months of that war. Its hero is Achilles, a mighty Greek warrior. *The Iliad* ends with the funeral of Hector, a Trojan hero who is killed by Achilles. The story tells of many heroes on both sides. One of the Greek heroes is named Odysseus. *The Odyssey* is named for him. In Greek, the title simply means "the story of Odysseus."

Odysseus is the king of Ithaca, an island off the coast of Greece. According to myth, Odysseus did not want to fight at Troy. He did not want to leave his wife, Penelope, and his baby son, Telemachus. He had to be tricked into joining the Greek army. Once he was involved in the fighting, however, he proved to be brave and clever. In fact, Odysseus thought of the trick that finally won the war for the Greeks.

You'll read about this trick in *The Odyssey*. However, the book is mostly about Odysseus' adventures after the Trojan War. In one adventure, he makes an enemy of Poseidon, the Sea God. Poseidon punishes him by making him wander the seas, never allowing him to reach home.

We meet Odysseus on an island, where he has been a prisoner for seven years. . . .

1 Athena and the Prince

Sing to me, goddess of song! Sing of Odysseus the Wanderer. Sing of the man blown this way and that, after he ruined Troy. Sing of the places he saw and the troubles he suffered. Begin now, daughter of Zeus! Tell the great story again!

By now, all those who fought the war and lived were safe at home—all but one man. His heart was on his wife and on coming home. The lovely nymph Calypso held him back. She wanted him as her own husband. At last, though, the gods took pity on him—all but Poseidon. The Sea God was away at the end of the earth. The other gods and goddesses sat in Zeus' hall on Mount Olympus.

"See how the mortals blame the gods for their troubles," said King Zeus. "Why don't they look to their own deeds? We warn them, and when they don't listen, they pay the price."

Then sparkling-eyed Athena spoke. "Father, let all die who bring it on themselves," she said. "But my heart breaks for Odysseus. He longs for his home and his loved ones. A goddess keeps him on her island. She tries to make him forget Ithaca. But he spends his days staring out to sea. He would be glad just to see hearth-smoke rising from his own land. Great Zeus, can't you pity him? Didn't he win your favor at Troy? Why do you hate him?"

"My child, how could I hate Odysseus?" said mighty Zeus. "He is the wisest of men. Great are his gifts to us who rule the skies. It's Poseidon who hates him. Odysseus blinded Poseidon's son, Polyphemus the Cyclops. Poseidon won't kill Odysseus but keeps him from reaching home. Let's think about this. How can we help Odysseus? Poseidon should not stand against the rest of us."

"Father, if it pleases you, I know what to do," Athena said. "Send Hermes to Calypso's island. Have him tell Calypso that you want Odysseus to go home. I will go to Ithaca and inspire Odysseus' son with courage. He must do something about the suitors—the men who wish to marry Odysseus' wife. They are living in his father's hall. He must seek news of his father and make his own name in the world."

Athena put on the sandals that carry her like wind over the earth. Down she swept from Mount Olympus. She stood, spear in hand, at Odysseus' gates. She looked like a warrior. The suitors were playing dice in front of the doors. They were eating Odysseus' cattle and drinking his wine.

The first to see her was Prince Telemachus. His heart was sad. If only his father would drop down from the clouds! Odysseus would drive these suitors away and take back his place as king!

"Greetings, stranger!" the prince said to the goddess. "You are welcome here." He led her inside. He took her spear and placed it on a rack. He called for servants to bring food and wine.

Now the suitors swaggered in. They feasted, drank, and called for music. Telemachus leaned toward his guest. "Who are you?" he said. "Where are you from? What brings you to Ithaca?"

The goddess told him she was a trader, an old friend of Odysseus. "I heard that he was back," she said. "I see that the gods still keep him away. I can tell you, however, that Odysseus is alive. He won't be gone much longer. Now tell me—are you his son? You look like him."

"Yes, I am his son," Telemachus said. "My father must be the unluckiest of men! How I wish he were here, at home with his family!"

"Still," said Athena, "the gods have given this house *some* luck. Look what a fine son they gave Penelope! But tell me, who are these men? Look at them, making pigs of themselves in your house!"

"Well, my friend, once this house was rich," said Telemachus. "Now the gods have changed our luck. It would be better if my father had died at Troy. All Greece would honor him. Instead, he's lost. Now the gods make new troubles for us. You see these men? They are nobles from nearby lands. Each one wants my mother to marry him. They won't leave until she chooses one of them. They'll eat our food until it is gone. My mother won't have any of them, but she can't bear to tell them."

"If only Odysseus would come home!" Athena said. "He would drive them from his halls. Still, there is something you can do. Fit out a ship. Go to Pylos and talk to King Nestor. Go to Sparta and talk to King Menelaus. They may have news of your father. If he is alive, brave it out one more year. If he is dead, think of a way to kill these suitors in your house. You are a boy no longer. It's time you were a man."

"Your words give me courage," Telemachus said. "Won't you stay and rest? Let me give you a fine gift, such as a host should give a stranger."

"No, I must go back to my ship," the goddess said. "Save your gift for my return. It will bring you a good reward."

With that promise, Athena left. The prince was filled with wonder. Surely this must be a god! He returned to the suitors, filled with a god's courage.

The great bard Phemius was singing of the Greek heroes and their journey home from Troy. Suddenly, Penelope appeared in the hall.

"Phemius!" she cried. "You must know other songs. Stop this one. It breaks my heart."

"Why, Mother," said Telemachus, "bards and their songs are not to blame if Odysseus is not home. Zeus is to blame. Now, go back to your room. Tend to your spinning and weaving. Keep your serving women working hard. As for giving orders, *I* am master of this house."

Penelope was amazed at her son. She went up to her room. There she cried for Odysseus until at last Athena sealed her eyes with sleep.

The suitors were praying loudly. They all had the same prayer—to be Penelope's husband. "You suitors are a plague on my mother!" Telemachus said. "Tomorrow you will all leave my palace. Feast in your own houses. Eat up your own food instead of wasting ours, or you'll see how Zeus will pay you back!"

For a moment, the suitors were shocked into silence. They had never heard the prince speak that way before. Finally, Antinous answered him.

"Well, Telemachus," he said, "only the gods could teach you to talk so high and mighty! Why blame us? It's your mother's fault! For years, she has promised to marry one of us. She says she will choose when she finishes weaving a burial cloth for Laertes, Odysseus' old father. It's all a trick. Every day she weaves, and every night she undoes her work. This is our answer to you, Telemachus! Send your mother away or make her choose one of us. As long as she holds out, we'll stay here feasting!"

Telemachus spoke with calm good sense. "Antinous, how can I drive my mother away? No, I'll tell you what I'll do. I mean to sail for news of my father. If he's alive, I'll wait for him. If he's dead, I'll come back and hold a great funeral for him. *Then* I'll give my mother to one of you."

Later, Telemachus walked alone on the beach. He prayed to Athena for luck and courage. She appeared to him in the form of Mentor, his father's old friend. "You are the son of Odysseus and Penelope," she said. "You can stand against these suitors. There's not one man of sense or goodness among them. Now, I'll help you fit out a ship. Get supplies for 20 men. I'll go around the town and choose your crew. We'll leave at once."

The suitors feasted in the hall. They made fun of Telemachus. "The gods help us!" one of them shouted. "He wants to kill us all! He's off to hire pirates. Or maybe he's just buying poison to put in our wine."

"Who knows?" said another. "He might drown like his father. What a boring job he'll leave us, dividing up his goods among us!"

"Even if he returns with Odysseus himself, what can he do?" said another. "Fight us all?"

Telemachus headed to his father's storeroom to gather supplies for his trip. He asked his old nurse,

Eurycleia, for help. He made her promise not to tell Penelope his plans until he was gone.

Athena, disguised as the prince, went into the town. She borrowed a ship and rounded up 20 brave young men. She hauled the ship down to the water. Then she went back to Odysseus' hall. She rained sleep over the suitors. Then, she became Mentor again, and she called out to the prince. "Telemachus, your crew is ready," she said. "They're waiting for your orders. Come now, no time to waste!"

Telemachus came with her to the harbor and found his crew waiting. "Come, friends, let's get the supplies aboard!" he commanded. When all was stowed away, they climbed aboard. Athena led the way, and Telemachus sat beside her. They cast off and raised the mast. Athena sent a strong wind over the wine-dark sea. The men poured out offerings to the gods. The ship went plunging all night long and through the dawn.

2 Meetings with Mighty Kings

At sunrise, the ship pulled into Pylos, King Nestor's city. On the beach, people were offering black bulls to Poseidon. They ate the meat, and they burned the leg bones for the god.

The crew pulled the boat up on the shore. They pulled down the sail. Telemachus climbed out last. "This is no time to be shy," Athena urged him. "We braved the seas for news of your father. Go to King Nestor. Ask him what he knows. He is far too wise to lie."

The prince was wise too, in his way. "Mentor, how can I speak to him?" he said. "Of course I'm shy— someone my age, addressing a king?"

"You'll find some of the words yourself," said the goddess. "The rest, the gods will give you."

Nestor was sitting among his sons. Pisistratus, a prince about Telemachus' age, came forward. He handed Athena a cup. "Say a prayer to Poseidon, friends," he said. "This is his feast."

Athena and Telemachus poured out wine to the god. "Hear me, Sea Lord, who holds the earth," they sang. "Bring luck to Nestor and his family and to all those here. Bring us safely home."

After they had feasted well, old Nestor spoke. "Who are you, friends?" he said. "Where do you come from? Are you traders or pirates?"

"Nestor, pride of Greece, I will tell you," said Telemachus. "We are from Ithaca. I seek news of my father, King Odysseus. Ten years ago, he fought with you at Troy. We have heard no word of how he died. Zeus hides it from us. Was he killed by an enemy or drowned at sea? That's why I've come. You may know something of his death. Please, if you do, don't hide the truth from me."

"Ah, dear boy, such memories you bring!" King Nestor said. "All those years at Troy! Nine years we fought before Zeus gave us victory. The heroes who died there—Achilles, Ajax, my own son Antilochus. Who could tell it all? No one there could match Odysseus for cunning. I can see you are his son. You have his way with words. No one so young could ever speak like you."

For hours, the king told his war stories. He spoke of the heroes who had come home. He told of King Agamemnon, murdered by Aegisthus, and how Agamemnon's son had taken revenge. "When a man is betrayed, how good it is to leave a son behind!" said Nestor. "You, my friend—be brave! People years from now will tell *your* story!"

Telemachus heard these words as a challenge. "I pray the gods would give me such power!" he said.

"I'd take revenge on those suitors who, without shame, invade my house!"

"I've heard about that crowd of suitors, my boy," said Nestor. "Who knows if Odysseus will ever return to drive them out. If only Athena would favor you, as she favored your father at Troy!"

"Never, your majesty," the prince said sadly.

"Telemachus!" said the bright-eyed goddess. "What is this nonsense? It's easy for a god to help a person—as long as he's alive. Once he's dead, though, not even the gods can save him."

"Please, Mentor, enough," Telemachus said. "I believe my father is beyond even the gods' help."

"My boy, don't stay away from home too long," said Nestor. "Those suitors will carve up everything you own. But if I were you, I'd go to Sparta. Visit Menelaus. He, too, roamed the sea for years after the war. Now he's home at last. Perhaps he has heard word of Odysseus."

Nestor invited his guests to stay the night in his palace. Telemachus accepted, but Athena chose to return to the ship. "I'll stay with the prince's crew," she said. "As Telemachus is now your guest, send him to Sparta with a chariot. Give him your finest horses. Let your son Pisistratus go with him."

With that, the goddess turned into an eagle and flew away. Everyone was amazed. The king took Telemachus' hand. "Dear boy," he said, "never be worried that you'll be a coward. Truly, this is Zeus' daughter, who lives on Mount Olympus!"

At dawn, they prayed and offered a calf to Athena. Then Nestor's youngest daughter dressed Telemachus like a god. Nestor ordered a chariot and horses for him.

It took Telemachus and Pisistratus two days to reach Sparta. King Menelaus was holding a wedding feast for his daughter. When a messenger told him two strangers had arrived, he invited them to join the feast.

"Look, Pisistratus," Telemachus whispered as he ate. "All this gold and silver, ivory and amber! Zeus' hall on Olympus must be like this!"

Menelaus heard him. "No man could match Zeus' power and riches," said the red-haired king. "Among men, though, few could match *me!* It took me years to gather all these treasures, and I rule them with no joy. While I was filling these halls, a stranger killed my brother. I mourn him and all my friends lost at Troy. Most of all, I mourn Odysseus. How they at Ithaca must mourn him, too— Penelope and old Laertes! There was a baby he left behind, too—Telemachus."

Telemachus cried when he heard his father's name. At this moment, Queen Helen entered the hall, looking like a goddess. Her women seated her beside her husband.

"Do we know, Menelaus, who our visitors are?" Helen said. "Surely this is Odysseus' son. I've never known two people who looked so much alike. This is the baby he left behind when you all went off to fight against Troy—to bring me back, though I did not deserve it."

"Yes, I see it, too," said the red-haired king. "How wonderful! My best friend's son, here in my own house!"

There were greetings, tears, speeches, and tales. Menelaus spoke of his own wanderings after the war. His ship had been wrecked in Egypt. There he had met a strange half-god, the Old Man of the Sea. Menelaus had asked this spirit which of his friends had come home safely.

"He told me," said Menelaus, "that Odysseus was still alive! He himself had seen Odysseus on the island of the nymph Calypso."

While the prince feasted in Menelaus' house, the suitors amused themselves with sports in front of Odysseus' palace. They threw the discus and the long spear. Sitting apart from the other suitors were the two strongest, Antinous and Eurymachus. The man whose ship Telemachus had borrowed came by. He asked innocently whether the prince had returned from Pylos.

This was how the suitors learned of Telemachus' plan. "Can you believe it?" Antinous raged. "He's gone to Nestor for help! May Zeus kill that boy before he's old enough to give us trouble! Let's get our own ship and crew. We'll wait for him off the coast. He'll end up the same place as his father—at the bottom of the sea!"

One of Penelope's servants heard them talking. He hurried off to warn the queen. The old nurse, Eurycleia, had told her where her son had gone. Penelope had been weeping and praying for his safety ever since. Now she cried out to Athena.

"Hear me, daughter of Zeus!" she cried. "If ever Odysseus honored you, help me now! Save my son from these gross, overbearing suitors!"

While Penelope prayed, Antinous was choosing 20 men. Down they went to the harbor. Penelope lay in her bed, weeping, refusing to eat and drink. At last, Athena sealed her eyes with sleep. Meanwhile, the suitors boarded their ship. They sailed to a small island and hid behind some rocks. There they waited to kill Telemachus.

3   Odysseus Rescued

As Dawn rose up from her bed, Zeus sent Hermes with a message to Calypso. "Tell her we want her to let Odysseus go," he said. "Let him build a raft and sail alone. He will reach the island of the Phaeacians. They will treat him like a god and send him home to his loved ones at last."

Down the clear, high air flew Hermes. He skimmed the waves like a bird. He reached land and walked to the cave where Calypso, the nymph with the lovely braids, makes her home.

Inside blazed a great fire of sweet-smelling wood. Beautiful trees of all kinds grew near the cave. Around its mouth was a vine heavy with grapes. Springs bubbled over meadows bright with flowers. Even a god could only gaze in wonder.

Then Hermes entered the cave. Calypso knew him the moment she saw him. As for Odysseus, Hermes could not find him there.

"God of the golden wand, why have you come?" Calypso asked.

"I'll tell you as one god to another," Hermes said. "Zeus sent me. He claims you keep someone here— one who fought at Troy and sailed for home. Zeus commands you to free him now."

The beautiful Calypso was angry. "You gods have no heart!" she said. "If a goddess dares to love a mortal, you become jealous. When Zeus crushed his ship, *I* saved him. The rest of his crew all died, but I brought him here. I would have made him a god! But how can I stand against Zeus' will? Let him go, then. Let him go."

Odysseus sat on the rocks. All day, every day, he sat on rocks and beaches, staring out to sea. "No more need to cry here," Calypso told him. "Don't waste your life away any longer. I'm sending you off now. Take tools and build a raft. I will give you food and water, wine and clothes. I'll send a strong wind to blow you home. This is the will of the gods, who rule the skies."

Odysseus shuddered. He gave a sharp cry. "Home? Never," he said. "I won't get on a raft unless you swear it isn't one of your tricks."

"I swear it by earth and sky and sea," she said. "I am planning no new trick to harm you. Good luck to you. Hurry back to your home and your wife, since you're so eager to do so. She must be lovely, if you prefer her to a goddess."

"Don't be angry with me," Odysseus said. "How can I compare her beauty to yours? She is mortal, and you never age or die. Even so, I long to be home."

The next morning, Odysseus started building his raft. He cut down 20 trees. He trimmed them and split them into boards. He drilled through them and fitted them together. He made the decks and set the mast. He added a steering oar and a sail. After four days, his work was done. It was as fit as any trading ship made by a master builder.

The lovely goddess sent him from her island. The wind sped the ship, and he set his course by the stars. Seventeen days he sailed. On the eighteenth, he saw mountains. The Phaeacians' island reached toward him over the waves.

Just then, Poseidon was returning from his journey. He saw Odysseus on the sea. "Look how the gods have changed their minds," he rumbled. "Just look at him—he'll be safe if he reaches land. I'll give him trouble yet!"

Poseidon grabbed his trident. Using the three-pronged spear, he rammed the clouds together. He whipped up the waves and the winds. As night swept down, the rolling sea tossed Odysseus' ship about. "What happens to me now?" Odysseus cried. "Why couldn't I have died at Troy with my friends, instead of like this?"

A great wave crashed down on his head. The ship spun around. The oar was torn from his hands. The mast broke. Odysseus was tossed into the sea. He fought to reach his ship again, but the winds blew it this way and that. Just as he put his hand on its side, Poseidon launched a huge wave. It shattered the boat into pieces. Odysseus jumped on one long board and rode it like a horse.

He rode the waves for two days. On the third, he saw land. A great wave rolled him toward the rocky shore. If Athena had not helped him, he would have been crushed. He grabbed for a rock and fought off the waves. He swam until he saw a sheltered place at the mouth of a river.

When Odysseus reached the shore, he struggled up the banks. He kissed the dry earth. Then Athena sent a great wave of sleep over him.

Odysseus had reached the land of the Phaeacians, where King Alcinous ruled. Athena went to Alcinous' house. There Nausicaa, the king's daughter, lay asleep.

"Nausicaa, you careless girl!" the goddess whispered. "You must wash your fine clothes in the morning. You are reaching an age to be married. Your clothes must look elegant for your wedding. I'll help you—the work will go fast."

Nausicaa awoke at dawn, wondering at her dream. Down she went through the house to tell her mother and father. She found the king about to leave for a meeting with his nobles.

"Father," she asked him, "could you get me a wagon? I want to bring our family's clothes down to the river for washing."

King Alcinous ordered a servant to prepare a wagon. Nausicaa piled clothes into it. Her mother packed a picnic basket for her and her maids.

The princess drove the mules to the river. She and the other girls scrubbed the clothes on rocks and spread them on the beach to dry. They bathed, smoothed their skin with oil, and ate their lunch. Then they began tossing a ball.

Athena acted again. The princess tossed the ball to a maid but missed her. The ball went splashing into a pool, and the girls all shouted out.

Odysseus woke. He sat up with a start. His heart was pounding. "Whose land have I found now?" he said to himself. "Are they cruel men without laws? Or do they fear the gods and treat strangers kindly? I hear girls shouting—or are they spirits? Do these people speak my language?"

Odysseus crept out of the bushes. He covered himself with a leafy branch. He moved out like a hungry lion about to raid a well-protected farm.

The girls saw him, all bloody and covered with salt. They screamed and ran down the beach—all except Nausicaa. Athena planted courage in her heart. Nausicaa stood and faced Odysseus.

"Are you a goddess or a girl?" he asked her. "Either way, I am at your mercy. If you're mortal, you must be a princess. How I envy your family!

What joy it must give them to see you dancing. Most blessed of all will be the man who marries you. I've never seen anyone like you. Please, be kind. The sea has brought me here. You're the only person I know here. Please, show me the way to your town. Give me a rag to cover myself. May the gods give you everything you wish."

"Stranger," the princess said, "you're a good man and no fool. Zeus has given you bad luck, but now your luck has changed. We are the Phaeacians. I am the daughter of King Alcinous."

She called to her maids. They gave Odysseus food and drink. After he had bathed in the river, they set out clean clothes for him. He had seemed like a monster when Nausicaa first saw him. Now he looked more like a god.

"Get up, friend," she told him. "Let's go to town. It's time you met my father and mother. They'll see you get what you want."

So Nausicaa led him to her home. Odysseus prayed to Athena that these Phaeacians would show him kindness. Athena heard him, but she still would not appear to him without disguise. The goddess was still worried about her uncle, Poseidon.

4 Among the Phaeacians

In front of the palace of the Phaeacian king is an orchard, four acres in size. Every kind of fruit grows there—pears and apples, figs and olives. The trees never die. They bear fruit in every season. Next, there is a field of grapes. Beyond it lies a great green vegetable garden. Two springs bubble up from the garden. One spring waters the gardens. The other rushes under the palace gates for the city people to drink.

Such were the gifts the gods rained down on King Alcinous' land. Odysseus gazed in wonder at all this plenty. Then he went past the gates and into the palace. Athena had placed a mist around him. It made him invisible until he was before the king and queen.

Nausicaa had told him all about her father and mother. Now Odysseus threw himself at the knees of the queen. The mist rolled back to reveal him. The men and women feasting in the hall fell silent.

"Queen Arete, I beg for mercy!" he cried. "May the gods bring riches on this house. As for myself, I ask for help getting home to my own country. I've been away from my loved ones for a long time. I have suffered greatly."

An old lord broke the silence. "Alcinous, your people are waiting," he said. "Come, raise this stranger up. Tell your servants to give us wine. We shall pour out cups to Zeus, who protects those who ask for favors. Give our guest his supper!"

It was done. The king gave Odysseus his own son's chair. He called for food and wine. After everyone had feasted, Alcinous spoke.

"Hear me, lords of Phaeacia," he said. "We shall meet at dawn and make offerings to the gods. Then we shall see about getting our new friend safely home."

Everyone cheered. They wished Odysseus well and went on their way. But Odysseus remained in the hall with royal Alcinous and Arete. The queen had noticed his clothes. She had made them herself for her own son. "Stranger, who are you?" she asked. "Where did you get those clothes? Didn't you say you came here by sea?"

"It would be hard work to tell you the whole story, my queen," said Odysseus. "This much I will say for now. There is an island where the nymph Calypso has her home. . . ." Odysseus told how he had longed to escape from the island and what had happened when he did. "When I woke up," he said, "there stood your daughter like a goddess. She gave me these clothes."

"So *she* gave you care and shelter!" said the king. "Friend, I wish you could stay with us and be her husband! Zeus would curse me, though, if I tried to keep you here against your will. Our men are the finest sailors. They will bring you home even if it lies at the end of the earth."

"May Zeus make it happen," said Odysseus.

At dawn, Alcinous led the way to the meeting grounds by the harbor. He and Odysseus sat side by side on a polished stone bench. Athena roamed through the town in the form of a messenger. "Come, lords of Phaeacia!" she cried. "Come to the meeting grounds! Meet the stranger who came here over the sea!"

Soon the seats were filled. The people gazed in wonder at the warrior who sat before them. Alcinous addressed his people. He told them how the stranger had come and what he wished. Then he ordered his sailors to prepare a fine, new ship.

"I want a crew of 52 of the best," said the king. "Have them fit out a ship with everything it needs. Then let all come to a banquet in my palace. Let's give this stranger a hero's welcome. We'll have the great bard, Demodocus, inspire us with song."

The bard was blind. He sat in a silver chair in the palace. After all had feasted, he sang a song of fighting heroes. Odysseus wept to hear his own deeds sung. Only Alcinous noticed his guest's tears. "Hear me!" he announced. "Enough of food and music for now. Let us go out again and test ourselves in contests. Let the stranger tell his friends at home what athletes the Phaeacians are!"

The people went out to see the games. The first event was a running race. It was won by one of the king's sons. Next came wrestling. A man named Broadsea beat all the rest. Then there was jumping, discus throwing, and boxing.

"Come, friends," said Laodamus, another of Alcinous' sons. "Let's ask our guest what sports he likes. Look at him—he's an athlete, all right!"

"Good idea," said Broadsea. "Go ahead, Laodamus, challenge him yourself."

The prince stood before Odysseus. "Come, stranger, won't you try your skill at sports before you sail?" he asked.

Odysseus spoke sharply. "Laodamus, why do you challenge me?" he said. "Troubles weigh on me now, not games. I only want to get home."

"I knew it!" Broadsea broke in. He grinned in Odysseus' face. "I knew you were no good at sports. You're a trader. You're only interested in gold. I can see that you're no athlete."

"*I* can see that you're a fool," Odysseus shot back. "The gods don't hand out all their gifts at once. Look at you—not even a god could improve on your looks. Inside your head, however, there is nothing. Your big mouth makes me angry. Look at me, worn down by troubles and pain. I've fought my way through the wars of men and the waves of gods. Even so, I'll give your sports a try."

Up he jumped. He grabbed the largest discus. He spun around and let it fly. The sailors waiting by the ship ducked their heads as it flew by. Athena, looking like a man, stood at the spot where it landed. "Look at that!" she cried. "It's so far past the others! There's no one who can touch you in this event."

Odysseus laughed, suddenly lighter in heart. "Match that, boys, and I'll throw one even farther. Any of you—come on, try me at boxing, wrestling, spear throwing, anything. I'll take on anyone except Laodamus—he's my host. Who'd be such a fool as to fight his friend?"

Everyone stood silent. Only Alcinous answered him. "Of course you want to show your gifts, my friend," he said. "You were insulted by a young fellow with no sense of fit speech. We're not great fighters, but Zeus has given us other gifts. We can race like the wind on land or sea. More important to us are feasting, music, and dance. We'll give you something to talk about when you feast in your own hall. Someone get Demodocus' lyre!"

Soon a stage was filled with dancers. Odysseus gazed with wonder at their flashing feet. At their center sat the blind bard. He sang a funny song of love and jealousy among the gods. Next, the island's two finest dancers put on a show that left Odysseus amazed. His praises brought cheer to the king and his people.

Alcinous called for the lords of the island to give the stranger gifts. First among them was Broadsea, who gave him a fine sword. The gifts were spread at Odysseus' feet for him to see. Then the royal guest was bathed and richly dressed.

On his return to the great hall, Odysseus saw Nausicaa standing there. "Good-bye, my friend," she said. "Remember me when you're home in your own land."

"Nausicaa, daughter of Alcinous, may Zeus make it so," Odysseus said gently. "Even at home, I'll pray to you as a goddess. You saved my life."

Odysseus took his seat beside the king. Wine was poured. Odysseus presented a choice cut of meat to the bard Demodocus. "Surely Apollo gave you your gift," Odysseus said to him. "You sing about the Greeks at Troy as if you had been there. Sing now of the wooden horse. Sing of the trap that Odysseus brought to Troy—the horse filled with fighting men who destroyed the city."

The bard sang of how the Greeks had burned their own camp and appeared to sail away. He sang of the wooden horse they had left behind and how the Trojans dragged it into the city as a prize of war. He sang of Odysseus' men, hiding in the horse's belly. He sang of Odysseus, fighting side by side with Menelaus, as they took the city. Odysseus listened to the song with tears running from his eyes.

"Hear me, lords of Phaeacia!" Alcinous said. "Let Demodocus rest his lyre now. I can see our guest is not pleased with this song. He has cried ever since it began.

"Now, come my friend," Alcinous said to Odysseus. "It's time we heard *your* story. Tell us who you are and where you come from. Where have your travels taken you? What people have you met? Tell us why you cry when you hear about the Greeks at Troy. Did you lose a son or a brother there? Tell us now."

5 The Cyclops

Odysseus, the great teller of tales, began his story. "Let me begin by telling you my name," he said. "I am Odysseus, son of Laertes. You know of my deeds. Ithaca is my home. It is a rugged land, but good for raising sons—and it's my own sweet country. Calypso tried to hold me back. She wanted me for a husband. So did Circe, the witch-queen of Aeaea. They never won my heart. Nothing is so sweet as a man's home country. . . .

"Enough. Let me tell you about what Zeus did to me as we sailed home from Troy.

"The wind blew us first to the Cicones' land. We fought against those friends of Troy. We burned their city and took much plunder. Was it enough for my men? Not for those greedy fools. There was too much wine to drink, too much meat to eat. The Cicones went for help. They brought a large force against us. Many men were killed. The rest of us barely rowed away with our lives.

"When we were almost home, Zeus hit us with the North Wind. Nine days we were blown south. On the tenth, we reached the land of the Lotus-eaters. The men there were gentle. They didn't try to kill us. They just gave us the lotus to eat. All who ate that sweet fruit forgot about going home. They just wanted to stay there forever and eat the lotus. I brought them back to the ships. I had to tie them to the rowing benches. We got out of there fast, before anyone else could eat the lotus.

"From there, we sailed to the land of the Cyclopes. They are monsters without laws. They know nothing of farming. They gather what they need of Zeus' plenty. They live in caves, each with his family, caring nothing for his neighbor.

"We found a harbor on an island near the Cyclopes' island. There were fruit and wild goats to eat, and there we rested. When Dawn, with her rose-red fingers, shone again, I called my men together. I wanted to learn what sort of men these Cyclopes were. I went across with my own ship and crew. The rest I ordered to stay behind.

"Just as we reached the Cyclopes' island, we saw a cave. Flocks of sheep and goats were kept in pens near the cave's mouth. A giant lived here—a monster, a man-mountain. He pastured his sheep far away and never mixed with the other Cyclopes.

"I left most of the men to guard the ship. I took only 12 of the best fighters and a skin of the finest wine. We climbed up to the cave. No one was there. We found cheeses, pails of milk, and lambs and goats in pens. My men begged me to take the food and leave. I told them we'd wait and see what the Cyclops gave us. So much the worse for my men!

"We built a fire. We offered some cheese to the gods and ate the rest ourselves. Then we sat back to wait for his return. Late in the day, he came with his flocks. He was carrying a huge load of wood to cook his supper. He threw the logs down with a crash. He pushed the female animals into the cave to milk and left the males outside. He closed his door with a huge rock. I tell you, 20 teams of horses could not have moved that stone! Then he sat down to milk and feed his animals.

"When he lit his fire, he saw us. 'Who are you?' he roared. 'Are you honest men or thieves?'

" 'We are Greeks,' I said, 'King Agamemnon's men, who destroyed great Troy. Since we've found you, we beg your welcome. It is Zeus' custom to treat strangers kindly.'

" 'You must be a fool, stranger, to threaten me with Zeus. We Cyclopes are not afraid of Zeus or of any god! We're stronger than the gods! Tell me, though, where is your ship?'

"I was not such a fool as to tell him. 'Poseidon of the earthquake wrecked my ship,' I said. 'My men and I barely escaped death.'

"The monster did not reply. He reached out and grabbed two of my friends. They wriggled like puppies in his hand.

38

"Then he smashed them dead on the floor. He ripped them apart and ate them, bones and all! We cried out to Zeus—it was all we could do. The Cyclops washed down his meat with milk. Then he stretched out on the floor of the cave and slept.

"My first thought was to kill him where he lay. Then I realized I'd be killing us as well. How could we ever move that huge stone at the mouth of the cave? So we lay there groaning until dawn.

"In the morning, the Cyclops milked and fed his animals. He did his chores. Then he grabbed two more of my men and had them for breakfast. He whistled as he drove his sheep to pasture. He lifted the huge stone to let them out, then slipped it back into place.

"How could I pay him back? Would Athena give me revenge? The Cyclops had left his club by the pens. It was big enough for a ship's mast. My men and I cut a six-foot length from it. We sharpened one end to a point. We turned it over the fire to make it hard. Then we hid it.

"In the evening, he came back herding his sheep. This time he brought them all into the cave. It was the same as before. After his milking and his chores, he ate two more of my men for supper. This time, though, I lifted up a bowl filled with wine.

"'Here, Cyclops, try this,' I said. 'It's just the thing to finish off your meal of human flesh. I brought it as a gift, you savage. You offend everything that's right!'

"The monster grabbed the bowl and drank. He liked it. 'More,' he growled, 'and tell me your name. I will give *you* a gift in return. We have wine here, but this is a drink for the gods!'

"I poured three bowls, and he drank them all down. 'You want to know my name, Cyclops?' I said. 'It's Noman. That's the name my parents gave me— Noman.'

"'Noman?' the Cyclops thundered back. 'Well, then, I'll eat Noman last of all his friends! I'll eat all the others first. That's my gift to you!'

"With that, he fell down drunk. He threw up chunks of human flesh mixed with wine. Then sleep came over him.

"Now was our chance. We grabbed the sharp pole from its hiding place. We made the point red-hot in the fire. We lifted the pole and drove it straight into the giant's eye. The men whipped it around with a strap, like a drill. The monster's eye hissed and burst. He let out a roar! The rock walls echoed. We fell back in terror. He clawed the bloody stick out of his eye and threw it aside. Mad with pain, he cried for help to the other Cyclopes.

"'What's the trouble, Polyphemus?' they called back. 'Is someone trying to rob or kill you?'

"'*Noman!*' Polyphemus roared back. 'Noman is trying to kill me! Noman has tricked me!'

" 'If no man is hurting you,' his friends called back, 'it must be Zeus. We can't help that! Better pray to your father, Lord Poseidon.'

"The Cyclops groped for the rock at his door. He pulled it aside and sat in the cave entrance. How could we get past him? I looked at the rams with their thick wool, and I had an idea. Working quietly, I tied the rams together with branches, three by three. Each ram in the middle would carry a man. The ones on either side would hide him. I tucked myself up under the belly of the biggest ram. There I hung, face up, holding on all night.

"When Dawn came with her rose-red fingers, the rams left the cave for their pasture. Their master now was shaking with pain. He felt the back of each ram as it went out. The fool never thought to check their bellies. Last of all came my great ram. Polyphemus stroked him gently and murmured, 'Dear old ram, why are you last to leave? You usually are first. Is your heart sick for your master? That coward—that Noman! If only you could tell me where he's hiding! I'd smash his brains out for what he did!'

"As soon we were out of the cave, I got free of the ram. Then I freed my men. We drove our flock to the ship and climbed aboard. There was no time to cry over the men we had lost. Once we were away from shore, I shouted up: 'That was no coward whose crew you ate, Cyclops! Zeus has paid you back for daring to eat your guests!'

"That only made the monster more angry. He ripped off a huge rock and threw it down at us. It splashed right in front of the ship and drove us back toward land! I grabbed a long pole and pushed us off again. Rock after rock he threw at us. My men begged me not to anger him further, but my blood was up. 'Cyclops, if anyone asks you who blinded you, tell him Odysseus did it! You hear that? Odysseus of Ithaca, Laertes' son!'

" 'I hear you!' he cried. 'Here is my guest-gift to you, Odysseus! Lord Poseidon, you claim to be my father. If it is true, see that Odysseus never reaches home! Or if he does, let him come home a broken man to a house full of trouble!'

"The monster threw one last rock. It nearly sank our ship. But the wave it made drove us to the island where our friends were waiting."

6 The Witch-Queen of Aeaea

"We came next to the island of Aeolus," continued Odysseus. "Zeus had made this king Lord of the Winds. Aeolus hosted me for a month. He asked for news of Troy and the Greek army. I told him the whole story. When I left, he gave me a sack. Inside were winds that blow from every direction. Aeolus tied the sack down inside my ship. He tied it shut with a cord and set the West Wind free to blow us home. He told us not to open the sack. Ah, but our own foolishness spoiled his plan.

"Nine days and nights we sailed. On the tenth, Ithaca came into sight. We could see fires on the beach. I fell asleep, tired from my work. That was when the men began to mutter. They were sure Aeolus' sack was full of gold. 'Look at our captain's luck!' said one to another. 'Everyone gives him treasure. We fought just as hard at Troy as he did! Hurry, let's see what's in that sack!'

"They opened the sack. All the winds burst out. A sudden storm blew up and swept us back to sea.

"I woke up with a start. I knew at once what had happened. I thought of jumping over the side and drowning myself. I chose to stay among the living. I hid my face from my crew as the wind blew us all the way back to Aeolus' island.

"The Wind Lord was amazed to see us again. Ashamed, I told him what had happened. 'Help me again, my friend,' I said. 'You have the power.'

"At first, our host was silent. Then he said, 'Get away from my island—fast! You're the most cursed man alive! Look at you, how you come crawling back! The gods must hate you! Get out!'

"We left the island with a heavy heart. The men's spirits were broken. They had to row—there was no wind to sail by.

"We rowed for six days and nights. On the seventh day, we reached the Laestrygonians' land. My men rowed right into the harbor and tied up their ships. I alone kept my ship outside.

"I sent three men to find out who lived there. They were invited into the king's palace. His wife was as huge as a rock on top of a mountain. She called her husband, the king. The king tore up one of my men for dinner. The other two escaped to the ships. The Laestrygonians came running. They were a race of giants! They threw rocks down the cliffs and smashed the ships to splinters. They speared the crews like fish.

"I pulled out my sword and cut the ropes that held my ship. 'Row for your lives!' I shouted at my crew. We got clear of the cliffs and out to sea. My ship alone escaped—all the rest were sunk.

"We were glad to escape death but sick at heart for our friends. Next, we reached the island of Aeaea. This is the home of Circe, the nymph who speaks with a human voice. Circe is the lovely and powerful daughter of the Sun and Ocean.

"We brought our ship into a harbor and rested for two days. On the third day, I went to scout out the land. I killed a deer and brought it back to my men. Once they had eaten, their strength returned.

"'Listen,' I said, 'I saw smoke rising from somewhere at the heart of the island.' This set the men to groaning. After the Cyclops and the Laestrygonians, who could blame them?

"I divided the men into two groups. I would lead one group. Eurylochus would lead the other. We drew lots from a helmet to see which group would set out first. The lot fell to Eurylochus. He led his men through the woods until they came to the palace.

"Wolves and lions roamed around Circe's walls. The men were terrified, but the animals did not attack them. Circe had tamed them with drugs. The men heard Circe singing inside as she worked at her loom. The house echoed to her lovely song.

"The men called out and greeted her. Circe opened her doors and invited them in. Eurylochus alone stayed behind. He feared a trap.

"Circe invited the men to sit at a table. She gave them food and wine, but into it she stirred an evil drug. It made them lose all memory of home. Once they had eaten, she hit them with a stick. They were pigs now, with snouts and grunts. Only their minds were still human. Circe herded them, squealing, into a pen. She fed them pigs' food.

"Eurylochus ran back to our ship. We pressed him with questions, but it was a while before he could talk. 'They all went in, Captain, but none came out!' he said. 'They all disappeared!'

"I took my sword and bow. I headed through the woods toward Circe's hall. As I came near, Hermes crossed my path.

"'What are you doing here, unlucky man?' Hermes said. 'Your men are all pigs in Circe's palace. Have you come to free them? You'll turn into a pig yourself. Wait, though, I have something for you. Take this plant. It will keep your mind clear when she casts her spell. When she hits you with her stick, draw your sword. Act like you're going to kill her. She will ask for mercy. She will tell you she loves you. Make her swear that she will do no more harm to you or your men.'

"Hermes pulled a plant from the ground and handed it to me. Then he flew away, back to Mount Olympus.

"My heart was a raging storm as I went up to

Circe's hall. I stood outside and shouted to her. She opened the door at once and invited me in. She placed me in a kingly chair and gave me her poisoned drink. I drank it down, but its magic didn't work. She hit me with her stick and said, 'Now, pig, off to your pen you go!' Instead, I drew my sword. I rushed at her as if to kill her. She screamed and dropped to her knees. 'Who are you?' she cried. 'No man has ever had power against my magic before! You must be Odysseus! Hermes always said you would come. Put away your sword now. Stay with me and be my love.'

" 'Circe,' I said, 'how dare you speak of love! You turned my men into pigs. You would have done the same to me! Now, goddess, swear that you will do no more harm to me or to my men!'

"So she swore, but I still would not eat or drink until she freed my men from her spell. I followed her out to the pen. The pigs stood facing us. She put a little oil on each of them with her stick. They turned into men again. They seemed younger and stronger than before. They all knew me at once. Each grasped my hands with joy. Circe stood there watching, a beautiful goddess now.

" 'Odysseus, king, Laertes' son,' she said, 'bring your ship up on my shore. Store your gear and your treasures in my caves. Bring the rest of your crew here. You will stay with me awhile.'

"So we did. My men were as happy to see me as if we had reached Ithaca. I brought them all to Circe's hall, where the feasting never ends. The men bathed and were given fresh clothes. The hall echoed with sounds of joy.

" 'Royal Odysseus, man of action,' said Circe, 'I know what punishments the sea has given you. Stay with me now. Feast well, and drink my wine. Let your men become as strong as when you first left Ithaca. Let courage fill their chests again.'

"So she won our spirits over. We stayed there in comfort for a year. When summer came again, however, my men grew restless. 'Captain, this is crazy,' they said. 'It's time you thought of your own home—if the gods really mean for you to reach your well-built house again!'

"That night, I told Circe that we had to leave. Our hearts longed to be home. 'I will not hold you against your will,' Circe said. 'But first you must go on another journey. You must travel down to Erebus, the House of Death. There you will speak with the ghost of Tiresias, the great blind seer of the city of Thebes. Even in death, he sees all. The rest of the dead are just empty shadows.'

"Her words crushed my heart. 'Circe, who can guide us on such a journey?' I asked. 'Who has ever reached the land of Death in a ship?'

" 'Odysseus, you were born for great deeds,' Circe

answered. 'You need no guide. Just spread your sail and let the North Wind take you. Cross the world-embracing river. You will see the grove of the goddess Persephone. Beach your ship there, where the River Styx flows down to the House of Death. Make offerings to the dead—milk and honey, then wine, then water. Sprinkle grain over it all. Promise the dead that when you reach Ithaca, you will make even greater offerings. Then kill a ram and a black ewe. Turn their heads toward Erebus. Have your men burn them and say prayers to the gods. The ghosts will swarm around you. Do not let them touch the sheep's blood until you have talked with Tiresias. He will tell you how you can reach home at last.'

"With these words, Dawn rose on her golden throne. Circe sent me on my way. I woke my men. I told them the course Circe had set. It broke their hearts, but of course their tears gained us nothing.

"Back to our swift ship we went. Circe had been there first. A ram and a black ewe were tied up close by."

7 In the House of the Dead

"Circe, the awesome, lovely goddess, kept her promise," said Odysseus. "A fresh wind sped us south. We came to the limits of the world. Ocean, the world-embracing river, was the land of the Kimmerian people. Here the sun never shines, and the land is always dark. We found the place that Circe had described and brought the sheep up on the beach. We made the offerings and promises she had told us to make. I killed the sheep with my sword and let their dark blood flow.

"Out of Erebus swarmed the dead. They were all around us. There were brides and young boys, old men and girls. There were great armies of men who had died in battle. I was terrified. I held my sword above the blood to keep them away.

"I saw the ghost of one of my men. He had drunk too much wine one night and fallen off Circe's roof. He begged me to remember him. I saw the ghost of my mother. She had been alive when I sailed for Troy. I cried for her—but I would not let her ghost near the blood.

"At last *he* came. 'King Odysseus, man of great deeds, what brings you here?' said the ghost of

Tiresias. 'Stand back—put up your sword. Let me drink this blood and tell you the truth.'

"I did as he asked. Once he had drunk the blood, his words came ringing as if he were alive.

" 'You seek an easy journey home, Odysseus, but a god will make it hard for you. You will never escape the Shaker of the Earth. Poseidon is angry because you blinded his son, the Cyclops. Even so, you and your men may at last get home—if you control them and yourself, too. You will reach Thrinacia. On this island, Helios, the Sun God, keeps his cattle. Leave the animals alone, and you all may still reach Ithaca. Harm them, and your ship and your men will be lost.'

" 'Even if you escape, it will take you years to get home,' Tiresias said. 'You'll be alone and broken. You'll find a world of pain. Cruel men will ruin your house and court your proud wife. You will pay them back in blood! Even then, you will have one more journey to make. Take your oar. Carry it far from the sea. You will find people who have never seen an oar, who don't know what it is. When this happens, plant it in the earth. Make offerings to Poseidon. Then go home and make offerings to all the gods. At last you will meet a gentle death, far from the sea. You will die a very old man, with your loved ones around you.'

" 'Tiresias,' I answered, 'surely the gods have

spun out this plan for me. But tell me this: I saw my mother here. She cannot look at me or speak to me. How can I make her know who I am?'

" 'That is easy,' said the famous seer. 'Any ghost you let come near the blood will tell you the truth. Anyone you refuse will disappear.'

"With these words, Tiresias' ghost walked back to the House of Death. I waited there until my mother came. She knew me at once.

" 'Oh, my son!' she cried. 'What brings you to this world of death? You are still alive!'

"I told her all that had happened since the day I sailed for Troy. I asked her then to tell me news of my people at home and of how she had died.

" 'Penelope still waits for you,' my mother said. 'Poor woman, she suffers just like you. No one has taken your place as king—not yet. Telemachus holds your lands in peace. Your father stays at his farm. He never goes anywhere. He is old. His grief grows as he waits for your return. It was the same grief that killed me. Yes, Odysseus—I died longing for you, my gentle, shining son.'

"I longed to embrace her, even though she was dead. Three times I went toward her. Three times she slipped through my fingers like a shadow. 'This is the way it is when we die,' she said. 'Life slips away from the bones. The spirit flies from the body like a dream.'

"We said good-bye. Then, slowly, there came a grand parade of the dead. First came women, all famous wives and daughters of princes. I could never name them all. . . ."

"But the time has come for sleep," Odysseus said to the Phaeacians. "The night is almost gone. Shall I sleep here in your palace or in the ship you have given me?"

"Ah, Odysseus," said King Alcinous, "you tell your story with a bard's skill. I say the night is still young! Tell me, did you meet any heroes in the House of Death—anyone you knew at Troy? Keep talking about your adventures. Your stories are wonderful! Tell us everything before you sail."

"Alcinous, there is a time for words and a time for sleep," said the man of great deeds. "But since you ask, I'll tell you. Yes, I saw Agamemnon's ghost. He told me what was done to him by his own wife and the murdering Aegisthus.

"I saw Achilles too, whom we Greeks honored as a god. I told him not to grieve about dying. 'There never was a man more blessed than you,' I said. 'Now you are most honored among the dead.'

"'Don't try to tell me about death, Odysseus!' Achilles cried. 'I'd rather be alive and the poorest slave than be king down here among the dead!'

"I saw others, too—Minos, son of Zeus, the great king of Crete. I saw Orion, the great hunter. I saw

Sisyphus, forever pushing his rock up the hill. I saw Tantalus in his endless torture. He stood in a pool with water up to his chin. His mouth was hot and dry with thirst. Every time he bent his head to drink, the water vanished. Fruit hung from branches above his head. Every time he reached for some, the wind would blow it out of his reach.

"I saw great Hercules, too. 'Son of Laertes, are you so unlucky as to be here alive, as I was?' he said. 'My troubles never ended—I, a son of Zeus! I was forced to slave for a man not half the man I was. He sent me down here once to bring back the dog that guards the dead. I did it, too, with Hermes' and Athena's help!'

"Then all the dead came crowding around me. Panic grabbed me. I rushed back to my ship and ordered the men to leave at once. Soon we were on the sea again. We rowed hard, and then a fresh, fair wind came up to speed us along."

8 The Cattle of the Sun

"The long waves carried us back to Aeaea, the land in the east where Dawn dances and Helios, the Sun, rises. Circe hurried toward us. With her were her ladies, carrying trays of bread, meat, and wine.

"The shining goddess greeted us. 'My dear, brave friends, who went down to the House of Death alive! Come rest with me today. Tomorrow you must sail again. I will set a course for you. Follow it, and no new dangers will trouble you.'

"That night, my men feasted and slept. Circe, though, drew me away from the others.

" 'Listen closely to what I tell you,' she said. 'You will come to the island of the Sirens. Don't get close enough to hear their voices in the air. Their high, thrilling song casts a spell. Those who hear it never see home or wife or children again. The Sirens lie in their meadow among piles of dead and rotting bodies. Race past their island! Plug your men's ears with wax so that none can hear them. If you insist on hearing, have your men tie you to the mast. Order them that if you beg to be set free, they must tie you tighter.

" 'Once past the Sirens, you'll see two great rocks.

One is tall enough to touch the sky. In that rock is a cave. Scylla lives there, a monster who scares even the gods. She has 12 legs and 6 heads on long necks. Each head has 3 rows of teeth. No ship gets by Scylla without losing a man to each head.

" 'Under the smaller rock lives Charybdis. Three times each day, she gulps down the water and spits it back out again. Not even Poseidon could save you from her whirlpool! Now, stay close to Scylla's rock. Row past as fast as you can. Better to lose six men than your whole ship!'

" 'Tell me, goddess,' I said. 'Couldn't I run from Charybdis and fight off Scylla?'

" 'Oh, brave hero!' Circe said. 'Are you so eager for battle? Can't you bow even to the gods? Scylla's not human—she's a savage force! You can't fight her! Just row for your lives!

" 'Then you will reach the island of Thrinacia. Here the Sun God keeps his sheep and oxen. They do not breed nor do they die. Leave the animals alone, and you all may still reach Ithaca. Harm them, and your ship and your men will be lost. Even if you escape, it will take you years to get home. You'll be alone and broken.'

"At these words, Dawn rose on her golden throne. Circe turned away. I went straight to my ship and ordered the men to cast off. Circe sent a wind to drive the ship and keep it on course.

" 'Friends,' I said to the others, 'it's wrong for only me to know Circe's secrets.' I told them about the dangers ahead and Circe's warnings.

"As we neared the Sirens' island, the wind died away. A strange power calmed the waves. The men plugged their ears with wax. They tied me to the mast. I could not move. Then they rowed.

"We were as close to the island as a man's shout can carry. Suddenly, the Sirens burst into their high, thrilling song.

" 'Come closer, famous Odysseus! Oh, pride and glory of Greece, bring your ship to us! Hear our song and sail on a wiser man! We know how you suffered on the plains of Troy! We know all that happens on the earth!'

"My heart raced to hear more. I signaled my men with my eyes to set me free. They only rowed harder. Two of them tied more ropes around me.

"Then the Sirens were behind us. I could no longer hear them. My men quickly pulled the wax from their ears and loosened the ropes that held me.

"We were no sooner past their island than I saw smoke and heard the roar of great waves. The men dropped their oars in terror. The ship lay dead in the water.

"I went around to each man to rouse his courage. I reminded the men that we had escaped the Cyclops. 'We will live to remember this someday,' I

told them. 'Take up your oars. Let's all work together and trust in Zeus. Keep clear of that smoke and the breaking waves. Stay near that big rock or we'll tip over into the whirlpool.'

"So I shouted. So they obeyed. I said nothing about Scylla, afraid that they would panic. I put Circe's advice out of my mind, though. It was not like me to run from a fight. I put on my armor and took spears in both hands. I stood forward on the deck. I looked for Scylla until my eyes ached, but I did not see her.

"Crying with fear, we rowed on through that narrow passage. Scylla was to our right. Charybdis was to our left. Her whirlpool was gulping down the sea. When she spat it out, the sea would explode over both great rocks at once. Now, though, the sea bottom lay bare. We could see rocks and black sand below. My men stared in terror at Charybdis.

"That was when Scylla grabbed six men from our ship. I looked back just in time to see them lifted in the air. They shrieked my name. They gasped and shook like fish pulled out of the water by a fisherman's line. Scylla swung them over her cliff and ate them raw. Of all the terrible things I have seen on the sea, this was the worst.

"Now at last, the monsters were behind us. We came to the good, green island of the Sun, the joy of human beings. Here was where Lord Helios keeps his cattle. We were close enough to hear cows lowing and sheep bleating.

"I remembered the words of the blind seer, Tiresias, and of Circe, too. I told the men about their warnings. 'They both told me we could find disaster here,' I said. 'Row right past this island!'

"It was Eurylochus who spoke up. 'You're a hard man, Odysseus,' he said. 'Your spirit is stronger than ours. You never stop fighting. You must be made of iron. Look at us! We're half dead. We need rest and good food. You're telling us not to land on this island? You want us to sail on by? Look, night is falling. Let's stop here and eat. We can be out to sea again in the morning!'

"The men cheered Eurylochus. I knew that this meant trouble. 'Eurylochus, I can't stand alone against you all,' I said. 'Just swear me this. If we come upon a herd of sheep or cattle, not one is to be killed or eaten. Just eat the food Circe gave us.'

"The men swore as I asked. We brought the ship into a deep harbor near a spring. We ate, we mourned our friends killed by Scylla, and we slept.

"During the night, Zeus sent a storm over us. We hauled the ship up on shore and put it in a cave. I warned the men once again to keep their hands off the Sun's cattle. Once again, they agreed.

"For a month, the South Wind blew. We could not leave the island. The food ran out. The men were hungry all the time. I went up to the middle of the island to pray to the gods for help.

"While I was gone, Eurylochus spoke to the others. 'Listen to me, brothers,' he said. 'To starve is the worst death of all. Let's take some animals from Helios' herds. If we ever get home to Ithaca, we'll build a great temple to the Sun God. If he means to wreck us over a few cows, I'd rather die that way than starve on this island!'

"So he said, and again his shipmates cheered. They drove off some cows that were grazing near our ship. They made offerings to the gods, killed the cattle, and cooked the meat.

"As I returned to the water's edge, I smelled the smoky smell of roasted meat. I cried out, groaning, to Zeus for letting this happen. Helios, however, burst out in anger against all the other gods.

" 'Father Zeus, all of you—punish them! Punish them all, Odysseus' whole crew! Those cattle were the joy of my heart! If I am not paid back in blood, I'll go down to Erebus and shine among the dead!'

" 'Sun, keep shining on the earth,' said Zeus. 'Those guilty ones will soon be on the wine-dark sea again. I'll tear their ship to splinters.'

"I heard this from the lovely nymph, Calypso. She said she heard it from Hermes.

"There was nothing I could do to set things right. The cattle were dead. The hides began to crawl like living animals. The roasted meat mooed! Yet my men ate it for six more days.

"On the seventh day, the wind dropped. We raised the sails and put to sea at last. Soon we were out of sight of land. Then Zeus sent a storm cloud out of the west. It tore off the ropes that held the mast. The mast fell, crushing one man. In the same breath, Zeus hit us with a bolt of lightning. The ship spun around and filled with fire. Men were pitched out and swept away by the waves. The god had ended their journey forever. I stayed with the ship until the sea tore it apart. I made a raft from planks and raised a bull's hide for a sail.

"I drifted for nine days. On the tenth, at night, the gods cast me up on Calypso's island. She took me in. She loved me. . . . I told you that story yesterday. You don't need to hear it again."

9 Ithaca

The next evening, Odysseus said good-bye to Alcinous and the Phaeacians. He asked the gods to bless his hosts. One last time, they offered wine to Zeus. Lastly, Odysseus wished health and long life to Queen Arete. Then he walked down to the beach. Food and wine were stored in the ship. A comfortable bed was made for Odysseus on the deck. He climbed aboard. The crew cast off. As their oars met the sea, sleep fell upon Odysseus.

The ship sped over the waves like a four-horse team speeding down the plain. Not even a bird could keep up with it. As the morning star rose, the ship reached land—Ithaca, at last.

The crew put in at a well-protected bay. They lifted Odysseus off the deck. They placed him on the sand under a spreading olive tree. Beside him they laid the treasures the Phaeacians had given him. Then they pushed off and headed home.

When Odysseus woke, he didn't know where he was. Athena had rained mist over everything. He thought he was on yet another strange shore.

Then Athena appeared, looking like a shepherd boy. Odysseus went up to her. "Greetings, friend," he said. "Tell me—where in the world am I?"

Athena's eyes were bright as she answered. "You must come from nowhere to ask such a question. This island is known the world around. The name of Ithaca has reached as far as Troy."

Ithaca! The name made Odysseus' heart race. At last he was home! He began to make up a tale about who he was and where he came from.

Athena smiled. Now she appeared as a woman. "Any man would have to be a champion liar to beat *you!*" she said. "Enough of this! As you are famous among men for your tricks, so am I among the gods. You didn't recognize me, did you? I am Athena. I have stood beside you during all your trials. Here I am to help you again. You are home now, but you must face more troubles in your own palace. Do not tell anyone who you are."

"Ah, goddess," said Odysseus, "you are hard to recognize. You take so many shapes! I know you were with me when we pulled down the towers of Troy. I don't remember seeing you since then."

"I was always with you," she said. "I could not bring myself to fight my uncle, Poseidon. I always knew you'd make it home, though. Look around!"

Athena lifted the mist, and Odysseus knew his home. He kissed the ground and wept.

Athena helped him hide his treasures in a cave. She told him about Penelope, Telemachus, and the suitors. She disguised him as a ragged old man. "Before you face the suitors, go see Eumaeus, the servant in charge of your pigs," Athena said. "He has been a loyal friend to your son and to Penelope. He'll tell you everything you need to know. I'm off to Sparta to call Telemachus home."

Odysseus climbed a steep path to the house of Eumaeus, the swineherd. A pack of dogs came snarling out of the yard. They would have torn him to pieces if their master had not called them off.

"You're lucky to be alive, old man," said the swineherd. "As for myself, I would have been shamed before the gods. Not that they haven't punished me enough! Here I sit, my heart broken for my master. I fatten up his hogs for those cursed suitors! Come inside, old man. Have some food and wine and tell me your story."

The loyal swineherd led his guest in. He gave Odysseus his own bed to sit on. The king was delighted. "May Zeus give you what you desire for the welcome you have given me!" he said.

"Every stranger and beggar comes from Zeus," Eumaeus said. "I'll kill a pig for your supper. It's just a skinny one—slaves' food. The suitors get all the fat ones. If my master hadn't gone off to fight at Troy, I'd have better to offer you! Now, *there* was a wealthy and generous man. . . ."

Odysseus ate and drank as Eumaeus praised him,

not knowing to whom he spoke. "Tell me," said Odysseus, "who is this master of yours? I've traveled the world over. Maybe I've met him."

"Ah, no," the swineherd said sadly. "Odysseus is lost and gone."

"My friend," Odysseus said, "I swear this to you: Odysseus *is* coming home! This very month, he will return. He will take revenge on any man who offends his wife and son. I swear it by Zeus!"

"Just as I wish," said the swineherd, "and Penelope, and old Laertes! Telemachus, too—the godlike boy! Speak of this no longer. It breaks my heart. Tell me your story, old soldier. Who are you? How did you get to Ithaca?"

Odysseus, the great teller of tales, began a new one. He came from Crete, he said. His father was a rich man, his mother a slave. He told of adventures in Egypt, but they were not his adventures.

Eumaeus now called for his men to kill their fattest hog. He offered the choicest pieces to the gods. His fellow slaves and his guest ate the rest.

That night, Odysseus slept in the swineherd's house. Eumaeus himself slept outside near his pigs. The swineherd took a spear to fight off men and dogs. He settled down to sleep under a rock that protected him from the wind.

10 Father and Son

Athena sped south to the hero's princely son. She found him and Nestor's son sleeping on great Menelaus' porch. At least Pisistratus was asleep. Telemachus lay awake, thinking about his father.

"You've stayed away too long, Telemachus," said Athena. "The suitors have no shame. They'll carve up all you have. Your trip here will come to nothing. Urge Menelaus to help you get home, quickly! You should know that some of the suitors are waiting for you in the channel. They mean to kill you. Land on the far side of the island. Go to the house of Eumaeus, the swineherd. Stay the night there. Send him to town to tell wise Penelope that you've made it home safely."

Athena went back to high Olympus. The prince woke Pisistratus. "Up, friend!" he said. "Hitch up the horses! Let's head for home!"

Menelaus was sorry to see them go. "I'd never keep you here against your will," he said. He would not let them leave without many gifts.

It was Helen, that shining woman, who gave Telemachus the greatest prize. It was a lovely robe, woven by her own hands. "This is for your bride to wear," she said. "Until you marry, let your mother keep it. May you return in joy to your country and your own house."

The horses galloped through the city and out into open country. On they flew, holding nothing back. On the second day, they came near Pylos. "Friend, I ask you a favor," Telemachus said to Pisistratus. "This trip has made us brothers. Don't drive past my ship. Leave me there. Your father loves being a host. I fear he'd keep me in his palace when I must hurry home."

Pisistratus agreed. He helped his friend load his ship. "Get away fast!" he said. "Be gone before I tell Father. Otherwise, he won't return to the palace without you. He'll be angry in any case!"

Telemachus called his men together. He gave orders to cast off. The sun sank, and the roads of the world grew dark. A wind from Zeus drove the ship on. As they neared Ithaca, Telemachus turned the ship away from danger—or so he hoped.

That night, Odysseus was again taking supper with the swineherd. "Listen, Eumaeus," he said, "tomorrow I mean to go beg in the town. Could you send someone with me as a guide? I may even go to King Odysseus' house. I'd like to tell Penelope my news that he's alive. Do you think those suitors will spare me a meal?"

"You are crazy!" the loyal swineherd said. "Those

suitors—even their slaves are a proud and violent group! No, stay here. You're not a burden to any of us. Wait until Telemachus comes back. He'll be kind to you." Guest and host talked far into the night. At last, they fell asleep.

As Dawn took her golden throne, Telemachus and his crew were arriving home. "Take our ship around to the city," he told them. "I've got to see how my farm is doing. I'll be in town later. Tomorrow, we'll have a fine feast."

Telemachus walked quickly to the farm. The king and Eumaeus were sitting down to breakfast.

"Eumaeus, I think a friend of yours is here," Odysseus said. "The dogs aren't barking at him."

Eumaeus was amazed to see the prince. He rushed to him and kissed his face. "You're home, Telemachus! I never thought I'd see you again!"

"Dear old man, I'm glad to see you," the prince said. "Tell me—does my mother still hold out, or has she chosen one of the suitors?"

"Surely," said Eumaeus, "she's still waiting in your halls. The poor woman! What a terrible life, wasting away the nights, weeping away the days!"

As Telemachus entered, Odysseus rose to offer him his seat. "Stay where you are, stranger," said the prince. "Eumaeus will find a seat for me."

After they had eaten, Telemachus asked the swineherd where the stranger came from. Eumaeus repeated the story Odysseus had told him. "I put him in your hands for care and shelter," he said.

"How I wish I could offer him shelter!" said Telemachus. "It's those suitors! I'll give him new clothes, a sword, and sandals. If you like, keep him here and I'll send up some food. I can't let him go down among the suitors, though. They would make fun of him. It would break my heart! Eumaeus, go quickly. Go to my mother. Tell her I'm home safely. I'll wait here. Tell nobody else. Too many people want to kill me."

Eumaeus left for town. Athena watched him go. She came to the house. She was a beautiful, tall woman. The dogs crept away in terror.

Athena caught Odysseus' eye, but Telemachus could not sense her. "Odysseus, old soldier, now is the time," she said. "Tell your son the truth. You and he must plan the suitors' death. I'll be right with you—I'm blazing for battle!"

Athena stroked him with her wand. He was an old beggar no longer—he was Odysseus. His own son gazed at him in wonder.

"Who are you, stranger?" Telemachus asked. "You must be a god! Be kind to us! We will give you offerings—"

"No, I am not a god," patient, great Odysseus said. "I am your father. I am Odysseus."

With those words, Odysseus kissed his son.

Telemachus' tears wet the ground. "No, I don't believe it!" he said. "You're not my father! You're a god! A moment ago, you looked like an old beggar. Look at you now!"

"Telemachus," said his father, "I am Odysseus, home after many troubles. It is Athena's work that changes me. She has that power. I will tell you later how I got here. For now, we must plot what to do about those suitors."

"What, just the two of us?" said Telemachus. "There are more than a hundred of them! Isn't there anyone who will fight beside us?"

"Just two," said the old soldier, "Athena and Zeus. Do you think that is enough?"

Telemachus answered carefully. "They are two great champions, but they live up in the sky."

"Trust me," said his father. "They won't hold off from battle when we face the suitors. Listen now: Go home in the morning. Mix with that cruel crowd. I'll come later, looking like a beggar again. No matter what they do or say to me, hold your peace! Try to reason with them. At my signal, gather up all the weapons in the hall. They'll be black with smoke. Tell the suitors that you're having the weapons cleaned.

Tell them too that you're worried a bloody fight will break out when they're drunk. That would shame them all. Just leave swords and spears for us. Athena and Zeus will do the rest. Now, one last thing: Tell no one that I have come home. Don't tell Laertes or Eumaeus, not even Penelope. We must first learn which of our people are loyal to us both."

"Soon, father, you'll know my courage," said his son.

While father and son made their plans, the ship from Pylos pulled into the harbor. The prince's crew sent word to Penelope. It happened that their messenger and Eumaeus arrived at the same time.

Penelope was sitting among her women. "My queen, your son is home at last!" the messenger announced loudly. Eumaeus, though, whispered his message. Then he left to return to his pigs.

The news shook the suitors. They crowded out of the hall and sat in front of the gates. "We'd better send out a ship," Eurymachus said. "Tell our friends waiting to kill Telemachus to come back, fast."

"No need for that!" Amphinomus laughed. He pointed to the harbor. "Look: they're here."

The other suitors went down to meet the ship. They led the crew off to a secret meeting.

"I can't believe he escaped us!" Antinous said. "A god must have helped him get home. Very well, we'll kill Telemachus here! If we don't, he'll rouse the people against us. We'll kill him and divide his goods among us—all but the palace. That goes to the man who marries his mother."

The suitors were stunned by this plan. Amphinomus broke their silence. "It's a terrible thing to shed the blood of kings," he said. "Let's first learn the will of the gods. If Zeus approves our work, I'll kill the prince myself. If he does not, we must hold back!"

The others agreed to this plan. They went back to the palace. Penelope was waiting in the hall with her women. A loyal servant had heard the suitors plotting and had told her.

"You, Antinous!" Penelope cried. "They say you are the best man your age in Ithaca. You're no such thing! How dare you plot my son's death? Stop, I tell you! All of you, stop!"

Eurymachus tried to calm her. "Wise Penelope, have courage! No man here would do such a thing! Your son has nothing to fear from us!" Even as he spoke, he plotted murder in his heart.

Penelope went to her room. She cried until Athena sealed her eyes with sleep. At Eumaeus' house, the prince and his father were sleeping, too.

11 Beggar in the Hall

When young Dawn with her rose-red fingers shone once more, Telemachus put on his sandals. He picked up his spear. "I'm off to see my mother," he told Eumaeus. "She won't stop crying until she sees me. As for you, take this stranger into town so he can beg a meal. I can't put up everyone who comes by. I have my own troubles."

"As you wish, my friend," sly Odysseus said. "Just let me wait until the day warms up. The cold morning could hurt these old bones."

Telemachus walked quickly into town. He went into his well-built palace. Penelope came downstairs. She threw her arms around her son and kissed him. "You're home, Telemachus!" The words flew from her heart. "I never thought I'd see you again! Quick, tell me—any news of your dear father?"

Telemachus kept his promise to his father. He told his mother only what he had heard in Sparta: Odysseus was alive but a prisoner on Calypso's island. "Now," said the prince, "go up to your room with your serving women. Bathe and put on fresh clothes. Pray to the gods. Promise them a fine offering if Zeus should let us have revenge."

As they spoke, the suitors were playing games in front of the palace. Meanwhile, the loyal swineherd and his guest were making their slow way into town. By the time they reached the palace, the suitors had trooped inside for dinner.

"What a noble house!" the king said. "It must be Odysseus' house! See how each building is connected to the next. The courtyard walls are topped with fine tiles. Those doors—how strong they are! No army could break them down. I hear the sounds of feasting. I can smell roast meat! What hunger there is in my belly!" As he spoke, a dog lying nearby lifted its head and thumped its tail. It was Argos, trained by Odysseus as a puppy. He was old and weak, but he knew his master.

The swineherd went into the palace. The first to notice him was Telemachus. The prince nodded and waved him in. Eumaeus picked up a stool and sat beside the prince. Behind him came Odysseus, into his own house. Anyone who looked at him saw an old, broken, ragged beggar. He sat down just inside the door. Telemachus prepared a plate of food. He told Eumaeus to give it to the stranger. "Tell him to beg from all the suitors," said the prince. "Shyness is no friend of a man in need."

The suitors pitied the old beggar. They gave him scraps. Then he came to Antinous.

"Prince, swineherd—why drag *this* in here?" said

Antinous. "Aren't there enough beggars here in town to eat your master's food?"

"Antinous, that was a low thing to say," Eumaeus said. "I wouldn't ask a stranger in unless he had some skill to serve the house. Who would invite a beggar in to bleed his master white?"

"Don't waste any breath on Antinous," said Telemachus. "That's just the way he is." He turned on Antinous. "What kind of advice is that? Drive a stranger from my door? Nothing we give this beggar will upset my mother—not that you'd notice. You're too busy feasting!"

"So high and mighty, Telemachus!" Antinous snarled. "I'll give him something, all right!"

Odysseus stood before Antinous. "Pity, sir," he said. "You look like a king. You should give me the biggest piece. You eat off another man's table. Why can't you spare me a scrap?"

"Here's what I'll spare you!" Antinous threw a stool and hit Odysseus in the back.

The other suitors were upset. "That was a crime, Antinous, to strike a poor beggar," more than one of them said. Antinous paid no attention. Telemachus said nothing, but his mind was full of bloody thoughts. Odysseus just shook his head. He went back and sat by the door.

Up in her room, Penelope heard how Antinous had hit the stranger. "May Apollo the Archer hit him just as hard!" she cried. "They're all hateful, evil men, but Antinous is the worst of all! Let death come down on every one of these suitors!"

While Odysseus ate his supper, Penelope called Eumaeus to her. "Send the stranger to me," she said. "I'd like to give him a warm welcome. Maybe he's heard news about my husband."

"Truly, he says he has," answered the loyal swineherd. "I'm sure he'll tell you face to face."

Eumaeus brought the queen's message to his guest. "I'll gladly tell your wise queen the truth," Odysseus said, "but I'm afraid of what those suitors might do. There seems to be no one here on my side. Tell the queen to wait until dark. Then I'll tell her privately all I know about Odysseus."

Eumaeus went back to Penelope. She agreed that the stranger was wise to wait. The swineherd returned to Telemachus in the hall. "I must go back to the farm," he said. "I have work to do. You must look after things here—especially your own skin."

"I will look after things," said the prince. "Come back tomorrow, and you'll see."

A beggar from the town was lounging around the palace. He was a huge man called Irus. At a signal from the suitors, he picked a fight with the stranger. "Get out, old man, before I pull you out by the leg!" he snarled at Odysseus.

"What have I done to you?" said Odysseus. "What

have I said? This doorway is big enough for both of us."

Irus kept on abusing him. Antinous, laughing, called to the other suitors. "A fight!" he said. "That would be fun! Let's match them up! The winner will be the only man allowed to beg here!"

Odysseus tried to talk his way out of it. The suitors pushed him forward. Then Athena did her work. Suddenly, the beggar looked like a boxer. "Will you look at the build on that old man!" the suitors cried.

Irus saw it, too. He was scared now. He tried to back away, but Antinous stopped him. "You fat ox, you're better off dead if you're afraid of *him!*"

The suitors pushed Irus forward. Both men put up their fists. Irus threw the first punch at Odysseus' shoulder. Odysseus hooked him under the ear, smashing his neck. Down went Irus. Odysseus picked him up by the leg and threw him out into the street. The suitors crowded around Odysseus, laughing and giving him food.

Then Athena inspired Penelope to go among the suitors. The goddess made her more beautiful than ever as she came down the stairs. The suitors' knees went weak. Her first words were to her son.

"Telemachus, where is your sense?" she said. "How could you let a stranger be abused in our house? Shame on you!"

"Mother, you're right," said Telemachus. "But how can I do the right thing with these suitors everywhere? If only the gods would beat them the way Irus was beaten!"

Eurymachus stepped over to them. "Penelope, my wise and lovely queen!" he said. "No woman can match you in beauty or good sense!"

"You're wrong," Penelope said bitterly. "The gods destroyed everything I was. They did it the day the Greeks sailed away to Troy. Zeus has torn away my joy. Look at me! It used to be that when men courted a woman, they brought her gifts. They didn't eat up what was hers!"

Odysseus glowed with joy to hear Penelope say this. Antinous took her at her word. At once he sent a servant to bring a fine present for her. The other suitors did so, too.

Night came. The suitors grew tired of insulting the stranger. At Telemachus' urging, they went off to bed. Odysseus and his son were alone in the hall.

12 The Queen's Guest

"Now is the time," Odysseus said. "Get the weapons out of reach. You remember what to say if the suitors miss them."

At once, Telemachus did as his father asked. He called to his old nurse, Eurycleia. "Dear one, lock the women in their rooms until I can put my father's weapons away," he said. "No one has cleaned them since he sailed away."

"It's about time," said the loving nurse. "You should take better care of your house and its treasures. Tell me, though, who will help you if the maids are all locked up?"

"Our friend here will," said Telemachus coolly. "Any stranger who is fed here must work."

The nurse did as she was told. Odysseus and his son carried off the weapons. Before them went Athena, lighting the way with a golden lamp.

"Father, look!" Telemachus burst out. "The ceiling is glowing! There must be a god here!"

"Quiet!" said Odysseus. "Don't ask questions. Go to bed now. I need to talk with your mother."

Telemachus obeyed. He went off to his room and slept. His father waited alone in the hall.

Soon Penelope came down with a servant. "Bring our guest a soft chair," she said. "Let him sit and tell his story." When he was comfortable, Penelope began to question him. "Stranger, who are you? Where do you come from?"

"My lady, you are famous on the earth," said Odysseus. "You are as praised as any king who fears the gods and loves justice. Please, then, ask me anything else. Just don't ask me about my past. I don't want to sit here groaning in your house."

"Once I was praised," she said. "That was before the Greeks sailed away for Troy. Now my life is pain. These suitors . . . I've led them on for years. I tricked them into thinking I would choose one of them. They saw through my tricks. Now I must marry one of them. Even my parents tell me to choose one. My son sees how they eat up what should be his. . . . But please, tell me who you are."

"So you must know," said the master of tricks. "Very well, I'll tell you." He told her that he came from Crete and had met Odysseus in the war. He wove enough truth into his lie that Penelope believed him. She wept as he described Odysseus' clothes and his favorite servant.

"Now, stranger, you are even more welcome here than before," said Penelope. "I made Odysseus those clothes. Odysseus . . . I will never see him again."

"My queen, do not cry or grieve any longer," the man of tricks assured her. "Odysseus is alive. I heard it from the mouth of a king. I swear by Zeus, Odysseus will be home this month!"

"Odysseus. Was he a man or a dream?" said Penelope. "The day that dawns today will be the last I spend in this cursed house. I shall announce a contest. Odysseus used to line up 12 axes and shoot an arrow through them all. If any of the suitors can string Odysseus' bow and shoot an arrow through all 12 axes, I'll marry him. I'll leave this lovely house where once I was a bride."

"My queen," said the man of great deeds, "do it today! Before any of them can handle that bow, Odysseus will be home with you!"

"I'm going to bed now," wise Penelope said. "You have been a comfort to me. Let me give you clean clothes to wear. Perhaps the suitors will not treat you so meanly. Let me call my women to prepare a soft bed for you and wash your feet."

"No need!" Odysseus answered quickly. "I'm not used to the soft life. If you have some old, trusted servant though, I'll let *her* wash my feet."

Penelope called for Eurycleia. The old servant led the queen's guest away. "I'm glad to wash your feet," she said. "I'll tell you why. You're so much like Odysseus! Your looks and voice . . ."

"That's what everyone says who has met us both.

We do look alike."

The old woman took a basin and began to wash his feet. Then she saw the scar on his leg. It was from an old hunting accident. The wound had been made by a boar's tusk when Odysseus was a boy.

The old nurse suddenly let his foot fall. Water spilled across the floor. Tears rushed to her eyes. "You *are* Odysseus!" she whispered.

Before she could call Penelope, Odysseus grabbed her and held her close. "You want to kill me?" he said. "Don't say a word to anyone!"

"Child," the old woman said, "who do you think you're talking to? I'm as solid as iron!"

"Then keep quiet and leave things to the gods!"

The old woman brought more water. She bathed Odysseus and rubbed him with oil.

Odysseus made his bed on the floor in the entrance hall. He did not sleep. He was thinking about the suitors and the fight to come. One man against many . . . how could he do it?

Then Athena was by his side. "Still awake?" she said. "What are you worrying about? You're home with your wife and son—the finest boy you could hope to have!"

"You're right, goddess," he said, "but how can we two fight an army? There's another worry, too. What if I do kill all the suitors, thanks to you and Zeus? Their families will seek revenge. How do I hide from them?"

"You're impossible!" Athena replied. "Don't you know I will guard you to the end? Even if 50 armies came after us, you would drive them off. So sleep. Your troubles will soon be over." With that, the goddess rained sleep across his eyes.

Dawn rose on her golden throne. Servants began to gather in the palace. They built up the fire in the great hall. Telemachus rose, strong as a young god. He put on sandals. He took his sword and spear down to the hall. Eumaeus arrived, driving three pigs for the day's feasting.

The suitors trooped into the hall. They were still murmuring of killing Telemachus, if the gods gave the right signs. They began once again to abuse the beggar who had come among them. Athena did not let them hold back with their insults. She wanted Odysseus angry.

Wise Penelope placed her carved chair near the door. She wanted to hear every word that was said in the hall. A fine dinner was being prepared for the suitors. A goddess and a strong man, however, were preparing a finer feast.

13 The Bow of Odysseus

It was time. Athena inspired Penelope to get the bow and the axes. They lay hidden in a storeroom. Odysseus had not taken the bow when he went off to war. He used it only for hunting.

Penelope lifted the bow off its peg. For a moment she broke down in tears. Then she took the bow and arrows into the hall. Her women followed, carrying a chest that held the axes.

"Listen to me, my overbearing friends!" she cried to the suitors. "Day after day you trouble this house. You say it's to win me as a bride. Very well, here I am to be won. This is King Odysseus' bow. I will marry the man who can string the bow and shoot an arrow through all 12 axes."

She turned to Eumaeus and ordered him to line up the axes. The swineherd cried when he saw his master's bow. Antinous turned on him. "You fool, you're upsetting your queen. Shut up or get out, but leave that bow here. What a test we have before us! It won't be easy to string *his* bow!" In his heart, however, he saw himself doing it.

Telemachus laughed. "Zeus has made a fool of me!" he said. "My mother says she'll marry one of you, and I laugh like an idiot! Look at her—she has no equal anywhere in Greece. You all know it. Come, let's start this game. I'll try the bow myself first. Let me see if I'm the man my father was."

Telemachus dug a trench in the floor. He planted the axes so that the holes lined up. He tried to bend the bow. He might have done it, but Odysseus stopped him with a look. Telemachus understood. "By the gods, I'm weak!" he said. "I'm too young to fight off any man who rises against me. Come, all of you. You're all better men than I am. Try the bow and see who wins."

"Let's go, friends!" Antinous said. "One after another, from left to right. You're first, Leodes."

Leodes picked up the bow. He tried to bend it but could not. "Friends, this bow will kill us all," he said. "We'll never win *this* prize! Just try it. You'll see the truth. Go after some other woman — someone you can win the old way, with gifts."

"Listen to you talk!" Antinous cried. "Just because you're too weak, you think we all are? Come on, who's next?"

One by one, the suitors tried to bend the bow. It was no use. They all failed.

Meanwhile, Odysseus led Eumaeus outside. "Listen," he said, "how far would you go to fight beside Odysseus? Suppose a god dropped him here out of the sky. Would you fight for him?"

"Father Zeus, let it happen!" said Eumaeus. "You'd see how I'd fight for him!"

"Well, then," said Odysseus, "I'm here. I'm home after 20 years. If a god should help me beat the suitors, you'll be like Telemachus' brother to me. I'll find you a wife and give you land. I'll build you a fine house beside my own. Look, here is the scar made by a boar's tusk years ago."

Eumaeus knew the scar. He broke into tears and threw his arms about his master.

"Come, no more crying now," said Odysseus. "Let's go back inside, one at a time. Here is what we're going to do. . . ."

The master entered his well-built house and sat down on his stool. Eumaeus followed him in. Just then, Eurymachus was trying the bow. He had no better luck than the other suitors had.

"It's a dark day," Eurymachus said. "It's not just losing Penelope that bothers me. After all, there are other women in the world. What breaks my heart is that none of us can match Odysseus. What a disgrace! We'll be talked about by men not yet born!"

"Nonsense," said Antinous. "Today is a feast day to Apollo. Who bends bows today? Let us feast and make offerings to the Archer God. We'll finish the contest tomorrow."

The others all agreed. They drank wine and

poured some out to Apollo. Then Odysseus stood.

"Listen, my lords!" he said. "You are wise to let the bow rest. Tomorrow the Archer will let one of you win. For now, though, could *I* please try the bow? Laugh if you will. I just want to see if I have any strength left in these old hands."

The suitors did not laugh. They were angry. "You're drunk, old beggar-man!" said Antinous. "Drink all you want, but stay out of our business."

Now Eumaeus picked up the bow. He began to carry it to Odysseus. The suitors burst out in anger. "Where are you going with that bow? You dirty swineherd, go back to your pigs!"

"Go on with the bow," Telemachus shouted to him. "I'm master here. If I decided to give our guest this bow, it would be my right."

This set the suitors to laughing. Eumaeus handed the bow to Odysseus. Then he called the nurse aside. "Good Eurycleia, Telemachus wants you to lock the doors to the servants' rooms," he whispered. "Stay inside, no matter what happens."

The old nurse did as she was told. Eumaeus ran outside to lock the courtyard gates.

Now Odysseus held the bow. He turned it over and over in his hands. It was still strong and true. With one quick motion, he strung the bow.

Horror swept through the suitors. Their faces turned pale. Odysseus plucked the string and

made it sing. He picked up an arrow. He fitted it to the bow. He pulled the string back, back. Then, sitting on a stool, he shot. He did not miss an axe from first to last.

"My son," Odysseus said to Telemachus, "your guest has not disgraced you."

Now Telemachus stood beside his father. His spear was in his hand. His sword was at his side. The suitors were amazed, but they still did not know what was coming.

Odysseus stripped back his rags. He fitted another arrow to his bow. "Your contest is over," he shouted to the suitors. "Let's see if Apollo lets me hit another target!"

Odysseus aimed again. He shot Antinous in the throat. Antinous fell to the floor, dying.

The suitors jumped up, cursing the stranger, searching wildly for their weapons.

"You dogs!" cried Odysseus. "You never believed I'd come home from Troy! You had no fear of men's revenge or of the gods!"

The suitors were terrified now. Eurymachus alone was able to speak. "If you really are Odysseus, I don't blame you for hating us," he said. "It was all Antinous' fault. He made us do it. I swear we will all raise a tax on our lands. We will pay you back for everything."

Eurymachus was the next man to die.

All the men in the hall could not fight the king,

his son, and their servant. Some of the suitors broke into a storeroom and got weapons, but it was no use. Athena stood with Odysseus. She sent the suitors' arrows off target. One after another the suitors were killed. Soon they all lay dead on the floor, like a fisherman's catch on the beach.

The king sent his son to get Eurycleia. She found Odysseus standing in a pile of dead men.

"Be glad only in your heart," Odysseus warned her. "Do not rejoice over the dead. Their own acts set the gods against them."

"Let me go tell your wife the news," the old nurse said. "Some god has made her fast asleep."

"Not yet," said Odysseus. "First we must clear away the bodies and clean up the blood. We will light a fire to make the house pure with smoke."

The old nurse went back through the palace to tell the loyal servants. They came out of their rooms, amazed. They all threw their arms around Odysseus. They kissed him and welcomed him home. Odysseus broke down and cried. In his heart, he knew them all.

14 Peace

Eurycleia was laughing as she climbed the stairs. She stood by the queen's bed. "Penelope, wake up," she said. "It's what you've dreamed of all these years! Odysseus is home! He's home at last, and the suitors are all dead!"

"Dear old nurse, the gods have made you crazy," said Penelope. "Why do you tell me this? Haven't I cried enough?"

"It's all true! Odysseus is home! The stranger who begged in the hall—it's Odysseus! Telemachus knew all about it! He kept it secret so that they could pay back those snakes! You should have seen him—like a lion beside his kill!"

Penelope's heart burst with joy. She jumped from the bed. She still could not quite believe it. If the suitors were killed, surely a god had done it. Odysseus was lost, far from Greece.

She came down from her high room. She stepped into the hall. There sat Odysseus, leaning against a column. One moment he seemed to be the man she remembered. The next, all she saw was a pile of rags.

"Mother," said Telemachus, "how can you hold back? Go to him!"

"Child, I'm too full of wonder," Penelope said. "I cannot speak to him or even look him in the eyes. If he really is Odysseus, though, we two will know each other. We have secret signs between us that no one else can know."

The long-patient Odysseus smiled. "Leave your mother here with me," he said to his son. "She will know me soon enough. For now, let us think of defending ourselves. We brought down many princes today. Their families will come after us. We must let the people think that Penelope has finally chosen a husband. The house must seem to be preparing for a wedding. The town must not learn of the suitors' deaths until we have slipped away to our lands. There we will see how Zeus can help us win."

Now he was left alone with Penelope. Athena finished her work. She crowned him with beauty. She made him seem like a god before his wife.

"Strange woman!" said Odysseus. "The gods have made you harder than any woman on earth! What other wife could hold back, when her husband has come home to her after 20 years?"

"Strange man!" said Penelope. "I'm not that hard! I'm not surprised at how you've changed, either. You look just like the man who sailed for Troy all those years ago!"

Then husband and wife held each other and delighted in each other again. She told him all that had happened at home while he had been gone. He told her all his adventures. Night passed, and Dawn rose again. While Penelope slept, Athena led Odysseus, invisible, out of town.

Hermes the Guide led away the ghosts of the suitors. He brought them to the House of the Dead. Agamemnon and Achilles greeted them there. The suitors traded stories with these great heroes. They told how Odysseus and his son had killed them all.

Odysseus, meanwhile, had gone to see his father. Laertes threw his arms around his son and cried. "Father Zeus and all the gods still rule!" the old man said. "The suitors' families, though—they will come at us in a pack!"

"Do not fear," said his son. "Let us go to your lodge. Telemachus and my loyal swineherd are there. They are preparing a meal for us." The two went home, talking all the way. Athena stood by, making old Laertes seem young and strong again.

As they ate their supper, however, news was spreading through Ithaca. The suitors' families gathered before the palace. They cried out in grief and anger. The father of Antinous was in tears. "All those fighters he led away to Troy—those brave men—they're all dead!" he cried. "Now he comes home and kills the best of our princes, too! Quick, let's get him, before he runs away!" They put on their armor and gathered for battle.

On Olympus, Athena spoke to Zeus. "Father, what is your plan?" she asked. "Will you make this war go on, or will you bring peace?"

"My child," said Zeus, "why ask me? Wasn't this *your* plan, to have Odysseus come home and take revenge on the suitors? Do as you wish—but here is what I suggest. Let both sides agree that Odysseus be king as long as he lives. Let the killing be wiped from their memories. Let everyone be friends. Let peace come to Ithaca."

Down flew Athena. Odysseus and Telemachus were again preparing to face an army. The goddess cried out in a voice that stopped all the fighters where they stood.

"Stop, you men of Ithaca!" she said. "Hold back from war! Make peace at once. You, Odysseus, master of great deeds—stop now! Your days of war are over!"

So the goddess commanded. So all obeyed. So the daughter of Zeus handed down peace for all the years to come.